MW01140106

Stars Are Like People

We appreciate your interest in our book.
To order copies, please visit
www.amazon.com
or www.booksurge.com or call 1-866-308-6235, option #6
Thank you!

Copyright © 2008 Teri Bellows & Illustrator Doreen McGrath

All rights reserved.

ISBN: 1-4196-4578-1
ISBN-13: 978-1419645785

Stars Are Like People

A first astronomy book for children ages 8-80

Written by Teri Bellows
&
Illustrated by Doreen McGrath

IN HONOR OF OUR FRIENDSHIP

While we like the five armed figure to represent a star, real stars are spheres, and look like circles in this book.

Stars are like people.

You were born, and your family came together to welcome you.

A star is born. It is created from gas and dust that came together in space.

You grow and get bigger too. You change and develop from an infant, to a child, to a young adult.

A star grows
and gets bigger.
It changes and
develops

A person eats food...

...pees, breathes out waste air...
...and poops what they don't use...

...and gives off heat energy.

A star eats hydrogen, poops helium, and gives off many different kinds of energy.

People are different. You got your color from your parents when you were born. Your size can be like your parents or others in your family.

Stars are different colors and sizes. The temperature of the star's surface gives the star its color. The size depends on the molecules that were there when the star was born.

Gravity keeps you on the ground.
It is a force that pulls everything
toward the center of our planet
Earth.

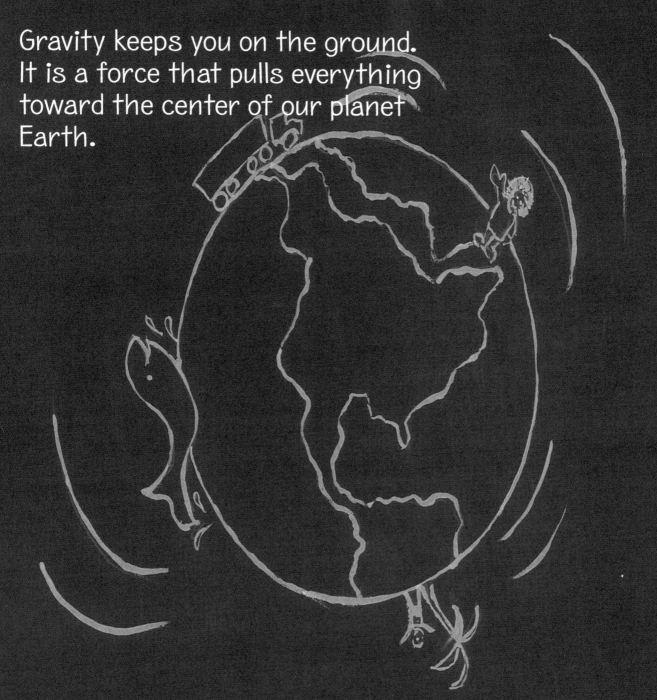

Gravity keeps a star together.
It is a pull to the star's center.

You could live to be 100 years old.

A star, like our Sun, will live to be
10 billion years old...
...and that is just an average
star lifetime.

When people die, their spirit goes to a better place, and they have a different life.

When bigger stars die, they explode, and their gases and dust go to a different place, where new stars are born.

Stars and people are made of the same stuff, and we share the Universe together.

Almost The End

Turn the page for astronomy information about the images in this book.

About the Illustrations Selected for this Book

NOTE: A light year is a measure of distance. It is the distance light travels in one Earth year. At a speed of 300,000 kilometers (186,000 miles) per second, light will travel almost 9.5 trillion kilometers (5.8 trillion miles) in one year! If you had to count the seconds to just one trillion, it would take you 32,000 years!

Temperatures are given in Kelvin. This is a scale that astronomers use, that is calculated by adding 273 degrees to the Celsius temperature. Since star temperatures are so high, there is not much difference between using Fahrenheit, Celsius and Kelvin scales. All stars are very hot balls of burning gas; never, never touch a real star.

Page 4: The Cone Nebula

William Hershel discovered the Cone Nebula in 1785. He is the same person that discovered the planet Uranus. The Cone Nebula is a region of space where new stars are forming. The red hue is produced by glowing hydrogen gas. It is located in the direction of constellation Monoceros, 2,500 light years away. That means when you look at the Cone Nebula, you are seeing it the way it looked 2,500 years ago, because it took that long for the light to reach your eyes. The stars are our future, but when we look up at the night sky, we actually are seeing the past!

Page 6: The Whirlpool Galaxy

This is a collection of over two hundred billion stars held together by gravity, in a spiral shape that is similar to our own Milky Way Galaxy. First discovered by Charles Messier in 1773, it is 23 million light years away in the direction of constellation Canes Venaciti. The Whirlpool Galaxy, 65 thousand light years across, is a bit smaller than our galaxy, but equally as beautiful, with many young, hot blue stars forming in its spiral arms. It was the first galaxy where the spiral structure was discovered, in 1845 by Lord Rosse. When a star system like our Solar System forms, it also looks something like this, with gas and dust swirling around a center point. The gasses in the center become the star, and the surrounding gas and dust can form planets.

Page 10: Rho Ophiuchi

Thanks to the talents of astrophotographer David Malin, many claim this nebula group to be the most colorful object in the sky. Small grains of illuminated carbon and silicon produce the blue reflection nebulae. Gas clouds of mostly hydrogen, excited by high energy starlight, produce the reddish emission nebulae. Neighboring red supergiant star Antares, in the constellation Scorpio, lights up the yellow and red clouds. Other dust clouds block light and appear dark for contrast. This is the most complete collection of nebula in one photograph. If you could travel to this area, in real life, it is even more colorful and intense and beautiful. The color of a star's surface indicates the star's temperature. Red stars are as cool as our Sun's sunspots (about 3,500 K) and blue-white stars are the hottest stars (20,000K and higher).

Page 12: The Cartwheel Galaxy

The Cartwheel Galaxy, 500 million light years away in the direction of constellation Sculptor, may have originally been a spiral galaxy like our own Milky Way. This unique shape that looks like a cartwheel was caused by a collision with a smaller galaxy. When galaxies collide, they pass through each other, but their gravity becomes distorted. The bright outside ring has massive, bright stars, newly formed from a shock wave of the collision. This wave is traveling out like ripples made in a pond, at about 200,000 mph, and formed the 100,000 light year diameter "wheel" pattern. This is one of the most amazing patterns made by gravity.

Page 14: Star Life Stages

These are the stages in a typical star's life. It forms in a contracting cloud of gas and dust, is cooler at first, and then gets hotter. At the end of its life it can expel outer gas layers and become a much smaller, but hotter, star. Smaller, cool stars live longer than bigger, hot stars.

Page 16: The Ring Nebula

From our place in space, we see a ring in the barrel-shaped cloud of gas ejected from the dying white dwarf star seen in the center. The Ring Nebula is 2,000 light years away in the direction of the constellation Lyra. The diameter of the ring is one light year across, and the colors of the gas indicate its composition of hydrogen, oxygen and nitrogen, and its temperatures: hot near the center and cooler at the edges. The temperature of the star in the center has been measured at over 100,000 K, and it is so dense that a teaspoon of the star's material would weigh over one ton.

1553765

Made in the USA